D0625055

## BRENT LIBRARIES

Please return/renew this item
by the last date shown.
Books may also be renewed by
phone or online.
Tel: 0333 370 4700
On-line  www.brent.gov.uk/libraryservice

*Richard Osmond*

# Useful Verses

PICADOR

First published 2017 by Picador
an imprint of Pan Macmillan
20 New Wharf Road, London N1 9RR
Associated companies throughout the world
www.panmacmillan.com

ISBN 978-1-5098-2419-9

3 5 7 9 8 6 4 2

A CIP catalogue record for this book is available from the British Library.

Printed and bound by CPI Group (UK) Ltd, Croydon, CR0 4YY

*For Jenny*

To conclude, fewe of them are good to be eaten; and most of them do suffocate and strangle the eater. Therefore I give my simple advice unto those that love such strange and newefangled meates, to beware of licking honie among thornes, least the sweetenes of the one do not countervaile the sharpnes and pricking of the other.

John Gerard, on mushrooms and toadstools, in
*The Herball or Generall Historie of Plantes* (1597)

# Contents

# Useful Verses for Distinguishing Cow Parsley from Poison Hemlock

*Cow parsley is of child height*
*and hemlock is a giant.*
*Above the barley, wheat and corn*
*hemlock stands defiant.*

Cow parsley stalks have a groove like the groove
in a stick of celery where the peanut butter goes.
Hemlock has a smooth hollow stem like a straw
through which if you drink you die.

*Hemlock from cow parsley*
*the blind man better tells.*
*Impossible to know by sight*
*the difference in smell.*

Green cow parsley seeds look like a supreme court
of alien slugs in tiny horsehair wigs.
Green hemlock seeds look like a handful of jacks
in the fist of an invisible boy.

*The stem of poison hemlock*
*is like a drunkard's skin:*
*purple blotches advertise*
*toxicity within.*

Dry cow parsley seeds are black cloven hooves, tapered
elegantly like those of sacred cows in Hindu frescos.
Dry hemlock seeds are Chinese sky lanterns crowding
the air above the funeral of one who ate hemlock seeds.

*Cow parsley is a bitter herb*
    *and hemlock it is sweet.*
*The taste of one will bother none*
    *if he the other eats.*

Cow parsley is the desire to restore to verse
something of its original mnemonic function.
Hemlock is a distracting preoccupation
with artifice and ornament.

*Cow parsley is of crochet made*
    *and hemlock is of lace*
*but a dead man won't know wool from silk*
    *as it's pulled across his face.*

# Huckleberries

That she lived
is now in the category of things
that are true
but may as well not be.

We kissed
only as Venus turns clockwise
or huckleberries
are the state fruit of Idaho.

# Luck and Colour

I caught a leprechaun in Braggot's Wood.
He was dressed in green
and wore a four-leaf clover on his belt.

His hat was the colour of Jack-by-the-Hedge.
His velvet blazer was the colour of nettles.
His trousers were the colour of cuckowes meate
or sleeping beauty. He was dressed in spring greens
and wore a delicious garnish on his belt.

His hat was the colour of *Alliaria petiolata*.
His velvet blazer was the colour of *Urtica dioica*.
His trousers were the colour of the leaves of *Oxalis acetosella*
or *corniculata*. He was dressed with precision and variety
and wore a quadrifoliate perennial on his belt.

His hat was the colour of oak leaves in May.
His velvet blazer was the colour of oak leaves in June.
His trousers were the colour of oak leaves in July
after the gall wasps hatch. He was dressed in a time and season
and wore the moveable feasts of Easter and Pentecost on his belt.

His hat was the colour of the Android symbol.
His velvet blazer was the colour of a Heineken label.
His trousers were the colour of www.paddypower.com's
trademarked background. He was dressed in strong brand identity
and wore a synergistic logo on his belt.

His hat was lighter than his velvet blazer.
His velvet blazer was lighter than his trousers.
His trousers were darker than his hat
and velvet blazer. He was dressed in a complex of small differences
and the plant he wore on his belt was divided four ways.

```
<html>
      <head>
              <title>Leprechaun</title>
              <style>
                      #hat  {color:#A3CD65;}
                      #vblazer  {color:#195407;}
                      #trou  {color:#003917;}
              </style>
      </head>
      <body>
              <div id="hat">
                      <p>His hat</p>
              </div>
              <div id="vblazer">
                      <p>His velvet blazer</p>
              </div>
              <div id="trou">
                      <p>His trousers</p>
              </div>
              <p>He was dressed in code<br>and wore a
              &#x1f340; on his belt.</p>
      </body>
</html>
```

I caught a leprechaun among
wood sorrel in Braggot's Wood
and demanded access to his pot of gold.

'Aha, good sir,' he said,
'the role that language and tradition
play in your perception of the rainbow
at the end of which I keep my crock
is not yet fully understood.
The location of my gold, therefore,
could well vary according to cultural bias.
Besides, your mesolimbic dopamine
circuit is stimulated by uncertainty.
The view of monetary gain as primary
motivator in, for example, gambling
addiction has now been superseded
by the theory that loss more strongly
reinforces compulsive behaviour.
Observe the lucky shamrock on my buckle,
which signifies both wealth and scarcity.
The reward you receive for catching me
depends on your not catching me
at least fifty per cent of the time.'

And then he disappeared.

# Inspiration

I wonder if the inventor
of the rotary drain snake,
which uses a corkscrew
action to find its way round
any corner, took the design
from black bryony, the sweet pea,
hops, grapes or another climbing
plant that grows by circumnutation,

a process by which shoots
grow spirally in the air
until they meet a branch
or stem and coil around it.

# Fire

Writing late, I fell a-microsleep and received the vision of a man on actual fire, dying in the street. When he spoke, the flames drew oxygen from his breath and flared in time with every word.

'Stop! I'm burning because you're reading the poem wrong.'

I slipped awake, unsure of how this followed. What poem? How could misinterpretation so directly immolate a person? I don't know, but figure I owe it to his blistered imaginary corpse to offer six possible explanations for what he said:

1: The man was Catholic and, despite the external flames, the fire he truly feared was that of Hell when he heard a young priest, newly ordained and flustered by emergency, butchering the Latin pronunciation of his last rites.

2: The inverse of the verse above, the man was deep into the occult – another system which sets enough store by true words properly intoned to explain his pleas to the unseen reader to read the poem right. Perhaps the difference between a voiced and unvoiced consonant is enough in necromancy to turn a charm for wealth and success into a curse for death by fire.

3: The dream took place within a poem and the flames the poet wrote were intended to be figurative, representing lust, and the man knew this and was understandably incensed to find his ardour literalised on the side of the road.

4: If we take into account how many poems have been read to how many listeners who did not burst into flames, the data point of this man's death becomes an outlier of such statistical insignificance that it requires no further investigation. Yes, for all we know it could happen again to any sufficiently unlucky listener to any poem anywhere but so could many things.

5: The poem took place within a dream created pharmaceutically by frustrated poets with an interest in lucid exploration of the unconscious who wanted to visit a zone where the metaphysical fallacy which drew them to verse in the first place – that the world is subordinate to words – held true. Imagine reading a poem inside itself, in the city made of language where every utterance is alive with a will and colour of its own. Imagine the potential and the risk.

6: The dream did not exist until you read this poem. I mean, it did but might as well have not until I made it into words. What comes in sleep stays asleep and the only dream that matters – the dream as told – is happening now, in your head not mine. Your eyes, after all, not mine, are moving rapidly back and forth to make images, as they do against their lids at night, of fire, in this instance, and subcutaneous fat bubbling under hot bloody flesh just like your eyes which, dreaming, seem to seethe and simmer under their thin covering of skin. Stop. By reading, you are killing him.

# High Fructose Corn Syrup

There is a sweetness in the air tonight
which these days barely qualifies as sweet.
When the total quantity of sugar
present in a drink like Dr Pepper
exceeds the upper threshold of humanly
appreciable sweetness by a factor of three,
what demand is there for sweet woodruff,
angelica, meadowsweet?

# The New Zodiac

The mouse fears the cat.
The cat fears the dog.
The dog fears the man.
The man fears the wolf.
The wolf fears lightning.
Lightning fears nothing.
Nothing fears a child.
The child fears the clown.
The clown fears the ringmaster
and ever since the incident
the ringmaster fears the elephant.
The elephant fears the mouse.

# Mugwort

Today, commuting down
the A13, I saw
a spike of mugwort
with blue-green leaves
with silver undersides
and a brick-red stem
growing out of the top
of a highly visible
traffic cone.

(*Artemisia vulgaris*:
relative of wormwood,
first named of the nine
herbs in *The Nine Herbs Charm*
and greatest among them:
adder banisher,
fish flavourer,
known as *una,* prime,
herb of herbs: symbolic
of symbology itself
and meaning the capacity
of herbs to mean.)

At thirteen, allowed
to go into town alone,
we hung out around
another traffic cone

in a walled garden
we were forbidden to enter
and did nothing. Or rather
we observed the tradition
that luminous signs removed
from their intended hazard
will congregate in waste ground,
borderlands, out of bounds,
wherever people loiter
and do nothing.

There is an age at which
every boy discovers
the potential of a can
of Lynx Africa
to make the Holy fire.
This was that age.
Someone whose name
I've forgotten sprayed
a whole can down
the circle-made-by-finger-
and-thumb sized hole
in the top of the cone
and lit the air above it.

To say I saw a phoenix,
or the gushing well
of Saint Alban, in whose
footsteps grew miraculous
flowers and from the ground

beneath each bounce
of whose decapitated head
flowed baptismal waters,
or a fiery premonition
of the unexpected
motorway mugwort plant
I saw today, bursting
like a bouquet from a wand,
would be to co-opt
other traffic cones
better left at their
respective accidents. Suffice
to say it meant something
to us then in that place
where we claimed most loudly
and often that nothing
would ever mean anything.

# Tradition

Nature is an anglerfish
    and memory her lover.
He fuses to her, flesh of flesh
    and never knows another.

# Disclosure

In addition to the Environmental Protection Act (EPA 1990) classifying all Japanese knotweed as 'controlled waste' and requiring that any growth be reported in writing to the proper authorities, homeowners are often asked to declare the presence of knotweed on their land to prospective buyers and mortgage lenders.

From *The Japanese Knotweed Code of Practice* (2013)

We collaborate on making and enforcing taboos
that may or may not benefit the commonweal.
For the good of my property's appreciating value
but not the health and diversity of our indigenous flora,
I will stay silent about Japanese knotweed,
with the obvious exception of this poem.
Consider the following stanza my only concession
to the law and a tacit alert to the Environment
Agency's department for harmful weeds and invasive
non-native plants, who may well read it someday
and, if so, will be free to act as they see fit.

*Trigger warning: graphic and lingering invocation of a dog's penis*

Spears of donkey rhubarb are burgeoning in my yard,
like the fleshy part of a dog's dick emerging
from its furry sheath, full at the base and tapered at the tip
like a lady's glove being pulled off by a loose pinch
of pink leather at the end of one finger, glabrous,
slick with a layer of faintly opaque mucus
and authenticated by a distinctive red craquelure
of broken capillaries all along the shaft.

# Metrical Charm to Cure Ear and Throat Ache

I had a fever
and a throat infection
which was causing a painful
pressure build-up in my Eustachian tubes.
Most nights I'd be woken by the throbbing
of my ears and tonsils.

One three-in-the-morning,
carrying the rationale of dreams
into my real bed, I found the pain was soothed
by repeatedly addressing each of my four
causes of discomfort by name in turn,
as if in meditation.
This seems reasonable enough
until you hear the names I used which,
for the duration of that moonlit time, seemed
to be the names by which I'd known these key players
in my upper respiratory system all my life.
From left to right, from my perspective
(that is left inner ear, left tonsil, right tonsil, right inner ear),
I addressed them as follows: Claire Hollywood,
Jethro, Maximus and Daniel Finkelstein.

One could analyse the glamorous
and feminine associations of left-handedness,
or bring to allegorical life the convenient marriage
of faux-ruralism and classical military force
in the American gun lobby of my throat

or remark upon the really quite hackneyed pun
made by my unconscious when it assigned a conservative
political commentator to an orifice on the far right
side of my head (though at the time I didn't know who he was),

but we must bear Stephen Pollington in mind
when he writes, in *Leechcraft: Early English
Charms, Plantlore and Healing*, that the way
an incantation works is often not,
as is also said of poems generally,
by employing the mnemonic properties
of rhyme and pattern to infuse
a ritual or remedy with greater and more
memorable significance, but quite the opposite:
some chants are perfect nonsense,
designed to render meaningless
the cause of pain or injury and return it
from the structured human body
to the unstructured chaos of the wild.

To follow the spell to its effective
end, I should have thrown
an artefact representing my disease
and misfortune across a busy road
or into fast-flowing water
and accompanied the noise
of traffic or the river's senseless
gabble with my own refrain:

*Claire Hollywood, Jethro, Maximus,
Daniel Finkelstein.*

# Riddle

A man sat drinking with his two wives, two sons, two daughters
and their two sons, the fathers of each of those sons, an uncle and
a nephew. Five people in total.

Old English riddle

My father and uncle lived in a windmill
with his wife, sister and daughter.
*Harold,* she'd say, *come to bed,*

but he was busy
making highbrow finger puppets
to entertain his one step-son from a previous relationship,
that is to say, himself.

Reader, how many, including me, sat
around our millstone breakfast table
as he tied himself in knots
doing the Sin/Death/Satan scene
from *Paradise Lost*
with only the digits of his left hand?

# Soon,

a yellow songbird, drowned in Armagnac,

Decades of
fluctuations
in humidity
cracked the
instrument
along its
sunburst
top pane
of cedar
wood. It
is finally
mended,
with ten
struts of
resonant
sitka in a
new and
diagonal
configuration, dividing
the underside of the sound board
into many diamond-shaped enclosures
with holes allowing the free exchange
of air, like how        the sealed hulls
on the Titanic       served to allow
the Atlantic its terminal access.
Grant Howe, my English luthier,
was detained for using a small mirror
on a telescopic arm to spy on women over
the wall of toilet cubicles. I admit I struggle
to compartmentalise the artist from his art,
but what commodity is sinless? He offered
me what I presume was the same mirror
to view those ingenious contrivances
which he installed inside my
mother's guitar.

# Osmepoeia

*To be read while smelling a sprig of Matricaria discoidea.
Inhale when you see this symbol:*

I've heard the unplaceable scent of this plant's
yellow buds and feathery, fragrant leaves compared
to green apple, olive, fig, bergamot, crab apple,
marmalade, plum, grass, lemongrass, lemon,
passion fruit, mango, parsley and fresh mown grass
but only by those who don't already know
its common name. For those who do, an ester
present here (probably ethyl butyrate), despite
being a component of innumerable possible aromas,
will evoke only one.

This phenomenon is best experienced by those
who are, like some of you, lucky enough
to be holding the flower to their noses when they first
hear its name and so can smell the function collapsing
in real time as the word learns itself into the brain:
pineapple weed.

Receptors in the nose do not respond, as was once
believed (in the 'lock and key' model of olfaction),
to the size and shape of molecules but to electrons'
vibrational frequencies at a quantum level. I know
that the uncertainty involved in such a process
is of an entirely different order from the experience
of being unsure as to what one is reminded of
by smelling a flower, and that any attempt to bring
the two into the final clinch of metaphor would be
guilty of an all-too-common category mistake

but we are in the poem, where thought tunnels
freely from one state and position to another.

# *Nina*

The bell, the ball,
the boot and the bone.
Nina taught me many things

not least the four distinct forms
of Chicken McNugget,
designed best to simulate irregularity.

# A Song for Gathering Daisies

Rice will be counted.
  Paper will be counted.
The wedding's never-ending but
  confetti will be counted.

The vampire is compelled to count
  everything he sees;
we scatter pennies on the grave
  to put our minds at ease.

A white baboon was picking ticks
  from the back of a white baboon
and that baboon was picking ticks
  from another white baboon

and each baboon picked ticks from every
  subsequent baboon
until the chain of monkeys reached
  halfway to the—

Daisy picking, plucking hairs:
  attraction and revulsion.
A tincture of the flower can be
  used to cure compulsion.

Whether I am loved or not
  is measured to a quantum;
that petal follows petal keeps me
  out of the asylum.

# Charm against Sleep Paralysis

*Translated from the Lacnunga*


Here he comes, creeping in:
a spider of a man to lash and bridle you
and ride you out across the fields.
He whispers in your ear

that you're his horse.
He drives you, dreaming, out to sea
until the water chills his urge
and he rolls over and falls asleep

and his sister takes his place.
Spooning you, she swears
to end your torture, whispering
in one ear and the other

that anyone who hears her charm
and knows the charm and chants
this charm, will not be sick,
suffer or be harmed.

# A Game of Golf

A <u>London bus, ty</u>res worn, slowed to a stop
on the road adjacent to the golf course
car park in North <u>London</u> where Don and I had
just parked his car next to three vintage Fords
(E-ser<u>ies, Cort</u>ina and <u>Escort</u>) and were ready to meet
Robert, our American client, fresh off the air<u>bus,</u>
<u>ty</u>pist in tow, from New York. For a game of golf.

As we were <u>escort</u>ed through the clubhouse,
Robert's ro<u>bust Y</u>ankee tones boomed above
the bar's hum. 'Elbow's a little stiff,' he said
on seeing us and mimed wearily lifting a <u>London</u> dry
gin to his lips, 'too many business lunch<u>es. Cort</u>isone
shot has helped my swing though, so don't go
too easy on me! And I got new clubs, coated with
Tef<u>lon – don</u>'t ask me what that achieves.
You guys eat? Waterme<u>lon? Don</u>ut?
Hungover? I'll have my assistant gra<u>b us Ty</u>lenol.
Sandra, would you go gra<u>b us Ty</u>lenol or whatever
they have here? Or are you guys still chewing on bark
for headaches? I'm kidding. If you were
you'd have better teeth. I'm kidding.'

Time passes. With the wind as its <u>escort</u>,
a single cumulonim<u>bus (ty</u>pical October
conditions in North <u>London</u> are much worse –
we were lucky to see the sun) moved

above the course. Below, around the birches,
honey fungus grew in bunches. *Cortinarius*
*violaceus* too, the purple webcap.
Later we would visit prostitutes and it would be no
big deal, but for now my putter was escorting the ball
from the land of the living into the blind netherworld
of the hole on the fifth green to dwell with the Greek God
Erebus, Týr of the Norse pantheon and all
deities of the void dead in their own mythology,
non-existent in ours or both.

I should explain my choice of words.
Robert was in town for a conference, a neurologist
now in pharmaceuticals and a lucrative client
of the marketing agency for whom my previous
project had been to co-ordinate the online presence
of a network of escort services and produce
copy optimised to rank highly in the results of Google
searches for the words 'busty London escort'.
I was tasked with curating entries on a blog
supposedly (but not actually) written by the wealthy
and successful customers of said busty London escorts,
detailing the aspirational and fulfilling ways they (the men)
spent their free time, including regular mentions of the busty
London escorts they frequented. The goal of these posts,
second to attracting traffic with both overt and cryptic
repetition of the keywords (a strategy which meant
the more successful posts in terms of traffic were liable
to descend into spells of profound nonsense), was to normalise
encounters with busty London escorts to such an extent

that they become no less acceptable a leisure activity
for doctors, bankers, lawyers and others of the executive
classes than the corporate golf games which so often
featured in their narratives.

It didn't reflect well on Don or the company,
which was on the verge of going bust (yearly
projections warned), that, having tactlessly beaten
Robert on the course, we returned to find the car
clamped. There was no parking in zones C or T;
they were reserved for the vintage Ford convention.

Hoping to salvage the afternoon with the promise
of erotic massage, I leaned close to our associate.
'On days like this,' I said, my speech taking on
the familiar cadence of a text whose intelligible sense
is subordinate to the working of some other automatic
process, like the arbitrary words which rush through a man's
head as he comes inside a woman who is not his wife,
'how better to unwind, Robert, bust your nut,
loose your felon dong or escape your fellow brain-
surgeons' incessant talk of cortices, cortices, cortices?'

## Lord, What A Morning

The cock crowed,
so I wrung its neck.

I prefer
to start my day
ambiguously.

# The Nine Herbs Charm

*Translated from the Lacnunga*

Remember, Mugwort, the revelation made
at Regenmeld when your reign began.
*Una*, they call you, first and oldest.
You heal thirty as thoroughly as three.
A boon to the blighted, you bury Black Death
and end infection which expands over land.

Mother Plantain, strong of a morning,
rising with the sun, resilient on the road,
carts have clattered over you and women cantered.
Brides have moaned on top of you and bulls blustered
but you withstood and withstand being stoned and stood-
upon just as you stand firm against
outbreaks which wound the world.

This herb is called Stune, it grows on a stone.
It banishes bane to overcome pain.

Next is Nettle, which never fails
to purge parasites and expunge pus.
Wort wages war against wyrm;
it wins against woe
and undoes the deeds of deadly disease.

Black Nightshade,
make less more and more less.
Balance lack and excess; bless
him burdened by one with a balm for both.

Cast your mind back, Camomile, to the deal closed
at Alorford: that any man who eats a meal
steeped in camomile will never suffer sepsis.

This is Crab Apple.
A seal sent it bobbing over the serrated sea:
foe to toxin and friend to all.

Nine plants for nine poisonings.
Once, a serpent snuck in and slit a man in half,
but Woden took nine wonder-sticks, whacked
the adder with each and split the snake apart
nine ways. Apple-twig met adder venom then.
That snake will never slither into someone's house again.

When the wise lord, heaven-holy, hung from the tree, he
made all the magico-medicinal herbs above
(and created Chervil and fashioned Fennel, the much-mighty duo)
and sent them to the seven worlds as tonic
and talisman against the fiend's hand,
false friends and withering curses cast by witches.

The nine herbs ward off nine demons who fell from heaven,
are antidotes to nine lethal doses, immunise against
nine airborne diseases and protect fully against the following:

white venom, sky-blue venom
yellow venom, green venom
brown venom, purple venom
night-sky-coloured venom,
sky-blue venom,

worm-blast, water-blast,
thorn-blast, thistle-blast,
ice-blast, poison-blast

and plague which drifts in from the East
or drifts in from the West,
or plague which drifts in from the North
and overtakes the Earth.

Christ did battle with the cruellest ailment, death,
but I alone know where a river runs
encompassed by nine adders.

Each weed must now spring up a wild herb.
Each scrubby plant must serve its purpose.
The seas will part –
salt water will slip free from itself –
when I break you from this curse.

# Roadkill

Passing Squamish
on the Sea to Sky Highway,
mosquitoes are dying against the screen
as countlessly as deer do in poems.

If this were a poem
we'd hit the biggest stag tonight
and pull over to learn ineffable truths
about chance and seat belts and being animal

but it isn't and we don't.
Yellow eyes in the dark stay in the dark
and the automatic wiper mistakes
the splatter of our small epiphanies for rain.

# *Fistulina hepatica*

The Holy Oak at Bruisyard first produced flesh
during the Feast of the Exaltation of the Cross.
Three bloody steaks burst from the lower trunk.
This was taken by the locals as an unequivocal sign
until the Peasenhall butcher returned home to find
a prime cut of his beef densely forested with tiny oaks.
The Lord giveth, and the Lord taketh away.

# Manna

Had nature an Iscariot,
That mushroom,—it is him.
Emily Dickinson

Lesser recognised and more feared
by the shopping public even
than the slimy toadstool, which
at least retains a recognisable
silhouette, tree fungus is
secretly delicious and I gather it.
A favourite is the beefsteak,
which grows like marbled
chunks of Christ's flesh from
broad-leafed trees and lends
a prized stain to the timber it infects.
Another fungus grows exclusively
on elder, the tree on which Judas was
believed to have hanged himself
and from which, if legend is indulged,
he still listens to the sins of man with gelatinous
purple ears. The first time I saw sulphur shelf
or chicken-of-the-woods bulging from an oak,
I was wrong to think it was a workman's
luminous yellow vest discarded at the roadside.
But a workman had been there nonetheless.
A yellow cross was painted on the tree,
presumably to notify the forestry commission

of the risk that edible rot would hollow out
and fell its host into oncoming traffic.
Since then, in shameful contrast
to the romantic ideal of foraging and
its slow communion with nature,
I search back roads and trash-filled
lay-bys from the car, braking hard
and dangerously at the first sign
of any tree that has been similarly defaced
and marked for removal. Like the first
of his profession – Jews of medieval
Europe who were forbidden ownership
of arable soil and forced to seek ghost meat
on no-man's-land and in the deep, decaying
woods – the mushroom hunter must become
acquainted with and be, himself, that which
society has symbolically condemned.

# Freddy's Revenge

During the bloody catastrophe of *Nightmare on Elm Street 2*,
which broke all the rules established by the original,

she let me get to third base. Crooking my fingers
like a Bavarian priest reaching up the chimney to bless a smoked ham,

I suffered a visitation from doubting Thomas
in a red and green striped sweater,

the colours of which, he whispered, had been chosen
for their disruptive effect on the visual cortex.

# The Sky God as Hell's Angel

*A horse-healing charm, after the second Merseburg incantation*

Woden, dipped in woad, a rider, rode.
Woad-dipped Woden rode a road bike
down the road. By dipped in woad
I mean tattooed. By road I mean road.

Woden, a bulky bearded God
in leather rode his warhorse of a
Harley down the road, his tattoos
sharing a societal function

with woad: to bond brothers,
strike fear and enshrine a law
and code firm and permanent
enough to be archived

on the vellum of an old man's arm.
Woden, dipped in woad, a rider, rode
his woad-encoded world down the road
until the bike broke down and slowed

but he yanked cranks
bodged dislodged cogs
wired wire to wire
and with white fire

welded well what needed
to be welded (to hell
with what did not)
and off he rode.

# To Nettles

A monk was partial to self-abuse
and so began daily to thrash
his dick and balls with nettles
in penance until

he developed a thing
for the stinging and spent
his days happily jerking it
to the hedgerow.

*To, for, over* or *about:*
with whichever pronoun
one follows the word
*masturbate,* we can agree
that the self-pleasurer and
the unknowing receiver
of his or her tribute
are linked by a dative
rather than accusative
relation.

I saw a patch of nettles
at the field's edge with
jagged leaves rich in
histamine and serotonin

to itch and inflame. Each
identical plant asserted itself
as individual or, more accurately,
I asserted them, every one,
in relation to my own concerns.

Each thing does not *selve*,
as Hopkins said, go itself,
but *others*, goes me, or I go me
in tangential regard to it
and its effects.

# To be entertained

is to be disappointed
and not realise.

# Amanita muscaria

At King's Cross, I saw men
in black hoodies with the words
*English Defence League* printed
in the colour and shape of the cross
of St George chase a suited man
onto a train and beat him, shouting,
'Nonce, you fucking Nazi prick'.

I did nothing,
but fixated on a map of the underground
on which the red typographical daggers
marked next to certain stations
seemed suddenly brutal and esoteric,
like burning Templar crosses.

Twenty miles north and three days later,
a ring of fly agarics disclosed
themselves to me in a wood of birches,
and the same hairs on my arm and neck
stood up like iron filings
in the presence of a strong magnet.

# The Rebus Principle

All those with questions
regarding metaphor,
I refer to Hunan province,

where a scribe of the Northern Song dynasty
is inking the sign for *scorpion*,
oracle bone script
having no character
for *ten thousand*.

# Association

*a retraction of a poem from my first pamphlet*

I wrote the following poem while recovering
from the minor operation elliptically described
in its first stanza: to cut the lingual frenulum
allowing the tongue greater mobility:

### Ankyloglossia

The sound of my tied tongue
being snipped free from the inside of my head
was like a child cutting snowflakes
out of thick sugar paper.
The association was involuntary

and I thought nothing of it
until later, when a show came on about a man
who had to live like a horse, with wild horses
on Exmoor
for three days and three nights.

The description of my procedure
and the image of the man and his ponies,
I told myself, exist in paradox:
proudly dissonant but necessarily related
by mere virtue of their selection and arrangement
in a poem, stitched and severed

by the gap between their stanzas
full of white snow or surgical wadding.

In reality, the lines that I pretended
were about being an abstract human poet and the loose,
illogical connections made possible by the gift of tongues
were about prescription painkillers.
Here's a missing scene which would have
made the whole thing unremarkable:

When the local anaesthetic started to wear off, aching up
the deep nerves in my jaw, I ate broccoli soup,
took two tablets of paracetamol with codeine phosphate
(500 mg/30 mg) and lay in bed watching iPlayer on my laptop.

The pharmacy has removed the traditional décor
of opium from its active alkaloids. Codeine,
lacking the jade pipes and dragon-embroidered silks,
carries a moveable aesthetic, which makes
a cushioned den or pleasure-dome of whatever
one is looking at or thinking when the pill kicks in.
For me it was the screen,
40 minutes into *My Life as an Animal*,
a ludicrous BBC Three reality show.

# Charm to Tame Wild Bees

*Translated from marginalia in Bede's Historia ecclesiastica*

Throw a handful of earth over swarming bees
and speak these words:

Simmer down, Valkyries. Go to ground.
Fly no more, wild, into the woods
but, bees, be mindful of livelihood.

You are my bag of yellow coins –
my herd of yellow cows –
honey is property.

## Alas, that very day, the King of the Elephants had eaten a bad mushroom.

As a child, I found one page of *The Story of Babar*
so disturbing that I would place a small palm
over the illustration as I read.
It showed the old king with crown askew,
no longer regal, weak, green and pitiful,
surrounded by scarlet amanitas.
He would have hallucinated as he died.

It occurs to me, crouching to identify *Paxillus involutus*,
the brown roll-rim, which contains variable amounts
of a cumulative toxin that can kill a person
after twenty years of eating the mushroom
with no apparent ill effects, that it is now my job to face
such poisonings unflinchingly – with aspiration even.
Some mushroom experts would have you believe
that they are safer and more enlightened than the general
population – more wise and cautious – but humanity
has never learned by any other means than fatal error.

To contribute anything of worth
to evolution, one must be prepared to follow
the good elephant's terrible example and die,
as my father did for me, in a unique
or memorably horrifying pose.

(Here, as we turn the page, the childish hand
of metaphor is lifted accidentally
from the true image of a once-strong man
dying of carcinoma of the lungs.
Don't look at him.)

# Meditation

Before we learned to pray the rosary
we used to shell broad beans.

# Red Berries

What would they say, I wonder, who believe
that girls like pink because they have
evolved to seek ripe fruit and pinch
the rosy cheeks of infants and boys
like blue because it is their imperative
to strive for the horizon, about the time

I was picking rose hips in the wood
where Potters Crouch Lane passes under
the A414 and found a set of Penelope Pitstop-
branded underwear (for girls aged seven to nine)
hanging from a hawthorn tree, having
clearly been soiled by a full-grown man?

# Charm for Clear Skin

*translated from inscriptions in a ninth-century*
*commentary on the psalms*

Pimple, pimple, little spot,
you shall not build here; you shall not
call this place (my face) your home
but instead must northward go,
to a hill not far from here –
to your brother's house, where
he'll put a leaf on your head.

By wolf's paw,
by eagle's claw,
by eagle's feather,
you will shrink away forever –
die like ash on glowing embers –
dry out smooth like plaster –
evaporate like summer rain.

Spot! Become a linseed grain
on a miller's fingertip:
no bigger than an inchworm's hip
and smaller than a thing so small
it isn't there at all.

# Sphinx

The golden eagle with a rabbit with myxomatosis
thrashing in its talons appeared to me
on a ridge outside Uig as the lateral solution
to a high-flown riddle no one asked

like what is fast, furred, slow and feathered? Or
what is alone in air and multiple on earth?
What is plague and deliverance from plague
and relief from deliverance from plague?

What has two tails, six legs, long teeth, keen razors,
golden plumage, pelt, two wings, two heads,
two eyes bloodshot and sticky with disease
and two eyes clear, immune and focused

on a man who like the true champion of *Jeopardy*
is working backward from the answer
and giving rising inflection to statements
which would otherwise be certain?

# Boletus edulis

The King has decreed
that bread be arbitrarily
scattered through the forest.

Any peasant caught eating
will be force-fed butter to death
and his corpse observed.

If the belly bursts with worms
before midnight of the harvest moon,
we go to war.

# Aphrodite and Eros

We had been swimming in Lost Lake, the one sandy beach of which
was crowded with people undressing or drying off. In front of us,
a young woman bent at the waist to finish wringing out her hair.
She faced away from me and her head was shrouded by a towel,
so I saw only the stretch of pale, smooth lower back exposed between
the waistband of her low-rise jeans and her damp T-shirt, which rode up
as she stooped.

(For skin to be perceived as soft, its dimensions must extend
along the axis of time. If you could creep between the seconds
like the owner of that magic stopwatch from *The Twilight Zone*
which froze the universe for all but its holder, or step inside
the image/moment complex of this poem [which works
in much the same way] and touch the woman's back, you would find
it unresponsive: as hard and cold as stone [heat, too, requires motion
and duration]. This was known to the sculptors of antiquity who,
working in frigid marble, expressed not only the form of timeless
beauty but its matter too.) She stood up

and I saw that the qualities of flesh and frame I had taken as belonging
to a slight and attractively boyish woman in perhaps her early twenties
belonged, in fact, to an actual boy of no more than thirteen, placing me
immediately in the same category as Samuel Pepys and Edgar Allan Poe
(who both married children) and the Ancient Greeks (who pleasured
themselves between the oiled thighs of pubescent servant lads) and all
other historical personages excused the tag of 'paedophile' today not
by their desires, which are totally consistent with those of the most
reviled in our society, but by the extenuating contexts within which
desire was performed.

# Chant

Hunters clothed symbolically in deer skin,
tracking deer, will look for grass on which
grow liberty caps nourished by the scat
of regularly grazing deer and wait.
Conversely, shamanic tribal elders,
hunting liberty caps, will search out deer,
the shit of which, on grass, breeds
liberty caps, and drop to their hands and knees.

Some advice is unhelpful to the point of being
a Zen meditation on the circularity of things.
Earth grows grass feeds deer make dung
engenders *Psilocybe semilanceata* conjures God
created the heavens and the earth grows grass.
Repeat while walking in a field at dawn.

# A Cure for Lunacy

*Translated from Bald's Leechbook*

If a man is moon-mad once a month, take
a porpoise from the sea and make the skin
into a whip and whip him with the whip
upside the head until he snaps out of it.

# Moonlight Usually Falls on the Image of Jenny

When we moved in together,
Jenny presented me with a traditionally
cross-stitched portrait of our
untraditional family: me and my antique
zither banjo, her and her American-English
red-tick raccoon hound, Presley.
By a quirk of the distance
between me on my side of the bed
and the small canvas on its shelf,
which makes the size of the grains
of video static speculatively fired
by my rods and cones when we
turn out the light coincide exactly
with the size of each individual
stitch in the picture, the embroidered
pixels seem alive and animate
with interference. This explains
the illusion of snow or rippling barley
but not the more complex patterns
I find myself selecting from the noise:
Moonlight usually falls on the image of Jenny
so she stays herself and still,
but what will happen outside
that pool of certainty tonight
is anyone's guess. Last night it was
a gang of archetypal grey aliens
lasciviously tugging at the hem

of her paisley dress. The night before,
a lion, rampant as in heraldry,
attacked. The night before that,
a midnight-blue cloak
swept about her like the sky
or death. Inevitably, though,
particulate randomness reasserts itself
over the half-illuminated
room and rain or sand
or dark fire consumes
everything – man, woman,
dog and instrument –
and I sleep.

# Terry Herbert

I think of him while picking winter chanterelles,
whose hollow stems resemble hilts
and bangles: flattened tubes of soft gold,
half bent by intent (the goldbender's art)
and half deformed by earth.

# Love Song, 31st July

Today the queen ant and her lovers
took their nuptial flight, scattering
upwards like a handful of cracked
black peppercorns thrown in the face
of a bear, the bear being in this case
a simile for the population of Lewisham
and Hither Green.

There is an increasingly common assertion
online that the winged of every ant nest
in Britain take off on the same bright
morning. This says less about ants than it does
about the state of media in which we place
ourselves: connected enough to hear
and repeat all claims and verify some,
yet prone to confirmation bias
owing to algorithms which favour
new expressions of that which we already
hold to be true.

Myth moves in step with commerce.
When merchant ships arrived
once per season from the Orient
they brought silk and saffron and stories
of dog-sized ants which mined gold
and took to the sky only to defend
their treasure from camel-riding

thieves. Now we receive the exotic
via fibre optics as a stream of
high frequency trades.

My love, I can't speak with authority
on commodity futures, the wonders of the east
and the behaviour of insects in Liverpool
and Tunbridge Wells or any city
outside my directly observable reality,
but it's flying ant day in my heart
if nowhere else.

# Bluegrass

*I.M. Earl Scruggs*

He played the banjo like a whiskey distiller
slitting open a sack of grain:
swiftly, with a workman's knack, spilling gold
in brilliant unquantifiable cascades.

In bluegrass we are moved
by no phrase in particular
but by the general principle
that small things in great number

behave as fluid.
He played the banjo
like a small boy in North Carolina
watching God move on the face of the cornfield.

## Acknowledgements

Thanks to Gerry Cambridge for publishing 'Freddy's Revenge' in *The Dark Horse*.

'Huckleberries', 'Riddle', 'Soon', 'Roadkill', 'Freddy's Revenge', 'The Rebus Principle' and 'Ankyloglossia' appeared in the 2014 pamphlet, *Shill*, published by HappenStance. Many thanks to Helena Nelson for the editorial input and support which shaped these poems.

The epigraph to 'Riddle' is a translation of an Old English riddle, the original of which can be found in the Exeter Book (Exeter Cathedral Library MS 3501).

The guitar-shaped poem is a caricature of both the form and conceit of Don Paterson's poem 'The Box' from his collection *Landing Light* (Faber & Faber, 2003). Thanks to Don for permitting this cheek.

'Charm against Sleep Paralysis' and 'The Nine Herbs Charm' are translations of Old English incantations found in a collection of Anglo-Saxon remedies known as the Lacnunga (BL Harley MS 585).

'Charm to Tame Wild Bees' is a translation of an Old English metrical charm found in the margin of Bede's *Historia ecclesiastica* (CCCC MS 41).

'Charm for Clear Skin' is a translation of an Old English charm found inscribed in pages added to a nineth-century commentary on the psalms (BL Royal MS 4 A xiv).

'A Cure for Lunacy' is a translation of instructions from an Anglo-Saxon medical text – Bald's Leechbook (BL Royal MS 12 D XVII).

The writing of *Useful Verses* would not have been possible without the inexhaustible patience, limitless excitement and formidable intellect of my wife, Dr Jenny Daggett. This book is for her, and for readers like her.